HAMPSHIRE
COUNTRY RECIPES

COMPILED BY
ANN GOMAR

RAVETTE BOOKS

Published by Ravette Limited,
3 Glenside Estate, Star Road,
Partridge Green, Horsham,
Sussex RH13 8RA
(0403) 710392

Production: Oval Projects Ltd.
Cover Design: Jim Wire
Printing & binding: Nørhaven AS

All recipes are given in Imperial and Metric
weights and measures. Where measurements
are given in 'cups', these are American cups,
holding 8 fluid ounces.

The recipes contained in this book are traditional
and many have been compiled from archival sources.
Every effort has been made to ensure that the recipes
are correct.

RECIPES

SOUPS, BEGINNINGS and SAVOURIES

Asparagus with Hollandaise Sauce 1

Cream of Asparagus Soup 2

Stilton and Celery Soup 3

Fish Soup 4

Careys Manor Vegetable Consommé
with a Julienne of Vegetable 6

Watercress Soup 8

Angels on Horseback 9

Devils on Horseback 10

FISH

Baked Mackerel with Gooseberry Sauce 11

Fordingbridge Lake Trout
with Cucumber Garnish and Fish Sauce 12

Dressed Crab 14

Salmon Mould 16

Salmon Pudding 17

POULTRY and GAME

Roast Venison 18

Casserole of Venison in Beer 20

Brockenhurst Baked Breast of Duck with
Demi-glaze Sauce 22

Tandoori Chicken from Pakistan and India 24

Chicken Curry from Bombay 26

Rabbit and Pork Hotpot 28

MEAT

Hampshire Rolypoly or Onion Roll   29
Beef, Lamb and Bacon Casserole   30
Hampshire Gammon and Apricot Pie   32
Isle of Wight Kidneys in Onions   33
Hampshire Kidneys in Onions   34
Carpet Bag Steak from America   35

CHEESE DISHES

Country Lemon and Strawberry Cheesecake   36
Little Cheese Custards   38

VEGETABLES

Brussels Sprouts with Cheese   39
Celery in Cheese Sauce   40
Baked Truffles   41
Hampshire Herb Pie with Marrow   42

PUDDINGS

Brown Bread and Honey Ice Cream   44
Stewed Pears in Red Wine   45
Winchester Pudding   46
Nelson Pudding with Apricot Sauce   48
Pumpkin Pie   50
Lemon Fairy Shape   52
Friar's Omelet   53
Blackberry and Apple Pie   54

Hampshire Pudding Pie or Gypsy Tart 56
Orange Jelly 57
Orange Custard 58
Boil'd Custard 58
Osborne Pudding 59

CAKES, BUNS and BISCUITS
Hampshire Drops 60
Mothering Sunday Wafers or Brandy Snaps 61
Original Doughnuts from the Isle of Wight 62
Mrs. Forster's Rich Seed Cake 63
Lardy Cake 64
Chocolate Sandwich Cake 66
Gingerbread Men or Husbands 68

PRESERVES
Rose Hip Syrup 69
Green Tomato Jam 70
Vegetable Marrow and Ginger Jam 71
Rowan Jelly 72
Red Tomato Chutney 73
Lady Sewell's Yellow or Green Cabbage Pickle 74
Watercress Spread 75
Apple Butter 76

STUFFINGS
Bacon, Celery and Apple Stuffing 77

SAUCES

Gooseberry Sauce   78

Homemade Tomato Ketchup or Catsup   79

Redcurrant and Raspberry Sauce   80

Hollandaise Sauce   81

Watercress Sauce   82

DRINKS

Elderflower Champagne   83

Grape Wine   84

HAMPSHIRE

The beautiful countryside of Hampshire, which is largely agricultural, varies from rich and fertile farmland supporting large herds of dairy and beef cattle, through rolling chalk downlands which are ideally suited to cereal growing, to regions of salt marsh, mudflat, woodland, forest and heathland. There are thatched villages with wonderful names like Nether Wallop, Middle Wallop and Over Wallop.

Hampshire is a large county with excellent market gardens and nurseries that produce soft fruit and vegetables, and is particularly famous for its luscious strawberries.

Many streams and rivers run south through the county to the sea, providing good trout, salmon and coarse fishing. The River Test is famous far beyond the county for its trout fishing, particularly near the town of Stockbridge. Salmon are caught in the river's lowest reaches below Romsey, and there is a famous salmon leap at the weir at Sadler's Mill, close to Broadlands, famous home of the late Earl Mountbatten of Burma, Admiral of the Fleet and last Viceroy of India. The 5,800 acre estate has one of the best pheasant shoots in the country.

Hampshire has a long and distinguished maritime and naval history, particularly connected with the historic ports of Portsmouth and Southampton and famous ships like Nelson's Victory, the medieval Mary Rose currently being restored after four hundred years on the seabed, the glamorous luxury liners, Queen Mary, Queen Elizabeth and QE2. The coastal waters are abundant in sea fish; bass, grey mullet, sole, mackerel, whiting, skate, cockles, mussels, winkles, crabs and lobsters are caught, and there are oyster beds in the rivers and around the coast.

The clear sparkling water of many of the rivers is good not only for trout but also for the growing of watercress, particularly in the Alresford region. Bunches of dark green, fresh watercress can be bought directly from the beds.

The Romans first introduced wine-growing into Britain, and recently vineyards have been successfully started again in the county, producing wines of excellent quality. Although hops are no longer grown, there were once large hop gardens on the fertile greensand near Alton. Travellers through the county by train could see, until the middle of this century advertising hoardings on the embankments reading: "You are entering the Strong Country". This was a reference to the local brewery, the Romsey-based company, Strong. Romsey has a reputation for brewing dating back to the 16th century. Drunken people were told "You must have been to Romsey".

Hampshire's county town is the City of Winchester. Once the capital of the Saxon Kingdom of Wessex and for some centuries capital of England, twenty kings are buried there. Its 15th century City Cross is known as the Butter Cross, because local women used to sell butter from its steps. Alfred the Great rebuilt much of the City. A huge bronze statue erected in a thousand years after his death, dominates Winchester's Broadway. The figure is set on a granite block, and it is said that in order to get an exact level, it was embedded in tons of demerara sugar.

The emblem of the county is the Hampshire Hog, the name by which a local inhabitant is also affectionately known. The weathervane by the West Gate in Winchester depicts a gilded Hampshire Hog in all its glory, indicating the importance of the pig in the economy and diet of the people. Small wonder that gammon and apricot pie is a favourite regional dish.

One of the county's best known areas is the New Forest, now one of the oldest remaining great forests in the country. First planted over 900 years ago, it was flattened by the Normans to create hunting grounds for William the Conqueror and his powerful nobles, burying, in the process, so legend has it, over 20 Saxon villages. The forest so created - and 'forest' in those days was defined as an area set aside for the sovereign's hunting - became a haven for wild life. Although wild boar no longer roam there, you can still see five varieties of deer, rabbits, hares, and the famous New Forest ponies.

The laws relating to traditional forest rights are administered by the Court of Verderers at the Queens House, Lyndhurst. One right, which dates back to Norman times, is that claimed by 'commoners', or people who live in the forest, to let pigs feed on fallen acorns in the autumn, called the pannage season. Acorns are green from September to November, and are excellent for fattening pigs, but they can poison other animals, including deer. Once they are brown and safe for deer and winged game to eat, the pannage pigs are excluded.

Sheep and cows also graze the forest, and blackberries, sloes, rowan and elderberries, mushrooms and if you are very lucky, truffles, can be found growing in wild profusion.

Hampshire is steeped in history - some connected with food and produce. In Tichbourne near Alresford a custom is carried out annually which was first started in 1150 by Roger de Tichbourne. The distribution of the Tichbourne Dole takes place on Lady Day, 25th March, from the church steps. The Dole, which used to be bread but is now flour, originated in the deathbed request of Roger de Tichbourne's wife. She asked that he give the produce from some of his land to help the poor. He agreed that the donation could come from as much land as she was able to crawl round during the time it took for a brand to burn. The brave lady crawled round 20 acres before dying, and to this day the land is called 'The Crawls' in her memory. Visitors to Winchester may ask for the Wayfarer's Dole of bread and ale, at the 12th century Hospital of St. Cross. The elderly pensioners who live in the Hospital almshouses wear flowing gowns and ruffled caps.

Today, Hampshire is still, as it has always been, a county generous with its hospitality, and rich in history and delicious food.

The mind of man is roaming free,
For novel beauty pants,
And this you'll find, now here, now there,
Within the range of Hants.

From *The Punster's Progress*
or *Villainous Village Puns*

ASPARAGUS WITH HOLLANDAISE SAUCE

Serves 2

20 thin sticks of asparagus - allow less per portion if the sticks are thick
Salt to taste

Wash the asparagus taking care not to break the sticks.

Cut off any woody ends, scrape the lower white parts lightly and trim the stalks to the same length.

Using soft string, tie the asparagus into two bundles of equal size.

Place the bundles, tips upwards, in a saucepan of boiling salted water - the water should come about three quarters of the way up the sticks, and the saucepan with the lid on should be tall enough to accomodate the asparagus. This will allow the tips of the asparagus which require less cooking than the rest of the stalks, to be cooked in the steam only, and therefore not overcooked.

Cook in boiling water with the lid on the saucepan for 15 to 20 minutes according to size.

Drain well.

Untie the bundles before serving with melted butter or Hollandaise Sauce (see recipe).

Eat with the fingers, dipping each stick into the sauce. The amount of each stick that can be eaten will depend upon the tenderness of the asparagus.

Asparagus is also delicious served cold with mayonnaise or vinaigrette dressing, or plain as a vegetable.

CREAM OF ASPARAGUS SOUP   Serves 4-6

1 lb (450 g) asparagus (tinned or inferior quality sticks may
   be used if preferred)
A little water
2 oz (50 g) butter or margarine
2 oz (50 g) flour
4 peppercorns
1 pint (600 ml/ 2$\frac{1}{2}$ cups) milk
$\frac{1}{2}$ pint (300 ml/ 1$\frac{1}{4}$ cups) white stock
1 small teaspoon of salt or to taste
2$\frac{1}{2}$ fl oz (4 tablespoons/ $\frac{1}{4}$ cup) cream

Wash the asparagus well, discarding any woody parts, and
cut the remainder into short pieces about 1 inch in length.

Put the tips into a saucepan containing enough boiling
water to just cover them.

Simmer gently for 10 minutes or until tender but unbroken.

Strain. Reserve the cooking liquid, and keep the tips to use
as a garnish.

Tie the peppercorns in a piece of muslin.

Put the rest of the asparagus in a saucepan together with the
reserved liquid, the peppercorns and the stock.

Bring to the boil, amd simmer gently for 20-30 minutes, or
until the asparagus is soft.

Rub the asparagus and the liquid through a sieve, or purée in
an electric blender.

Melt the fat in a saucepan.

Stir in the flour to make a roux. Still stirring, cook for a
few minutes, gradually adding the milk. Bring to the boil,
and cook gently until the mixture thickens.

Allow to cool slightly.

Stir in the asparagus purée and the cream.

Heat again and serve garnished with the asparagus tips.

STILTON AND CELERY SOUP

Serves 6

This delicious soup was 'a speciality of the house' at a public house, renowned for good fare, in Alresford.

1¹/₂ pints (900 ml/ 3³/₄ cups) chicken stock
7 oz (200 g) Blue Stilton cheese
4 sticks celery
1 large onion
A pinch of thyme
1¹/₂ oz (40 g) butter
1¹/₂ oz (40 g) plain flour
Salt and pepper to taste

Peel and chop the onion.

Melt the butter in a frying pan, and fry the onion until soft.

Chop the prepared celery.

Add to the onion, and continue cooking for a few minutes.

Add the flour and cook gently for 1 minute, stirring.

Pour on the stock gradually, stirring continuously.

Bring to the boil, then simmer for about 15 minutes or until the celery is cooked.

Grate the cheese, and add it to the soup, stirring until it is melted.

Add the thyme, and season with salt and pepper to taste. As the cheese is salty, only a very little salt will be required.

Cook the soup gently for a further 5 minutes.

Allow to cool.

Put through a sieve or liquidise in an electric blender.

Reheat before serving with crusty bread.

FISH SOUP FROM
THE ISLE OF WIGHT

All the towns in the Isle of Wight, with the exception of Newport in the centre, are on the coast. Fishing and agriculture are important industries, as is tourism. Visitors to the Isle of Wight are known to the locals as 'overners'.

At St. Catherine's Point at the island's southernmost tip the remains of two disused lighthouses are known as the Mustard Pot and the Pepper Box. Smuggling flourished on the island until well into the 19th century.

1 lb (450 g) white fish
1 onion
1 leek
1 stick of celery
Salt and pepper
2 tablespoons tomato purée
$^1/_2$ glass dry white wine
1 oz (25 g) flour
$^1/_4$ pint (150 ml/ $^2/_3$ cup) milk
A clove of garlic (optional)
1 oz (25 g) chopped parsley
4 tablespoons ($2^1/_2$ fl oz/ $^1/_3$ cup) single cream

Wash and roughly chop the onion, leek and celery.

Put the vegetables with the fish into a saucepan.

Add $1^1/_2$ pints (900 ml/ 3 cups) water.

Season to taste with salt and pepper.

Bring to the boil and simmer until fish is cooked.

Take the fish out of the pan, and remove the skin and bones.

Return the skin and bones to the stock and simmer for a further 15-20 minutes.

Meanwhile cut up the fish into bite-sized pieces.

Strain the stock through a fine sieve and return it to the pan.

Add the tomato purée and the white wine.

Mix the flour with the milk, and use to thicken the stock.

Simmer for a few minutes, stirring constantly.

Add the fish and crushed garlic if liked.

Stir in the cream lightly just before serving.

Heat through, but do not boil.

Serve hot with crusty bread, and garnished with chopped parsley.

VEGETABLE CONSOMME FROM CAREYS MANOR WITH A JULIENNE OF VEGETABLES

Serves 10

Careys Manor Hotel in the New Forest village of Brockenhurst, is a lovely old manor house with a modern garden wing and a reputation for good food. The village itself, with its thatched cottages and a ford across its main street, is equally attractive.

For the vegetable consommé:
4^1/$_2$ lbs (2 kg) roughly cut root vegetables
^{1}/$_2$ lb (225 g) field mushrooms
4 pints (2.25 litres/ 8 cups) cold water
6 egg whites
Bouquet garni
Salt and pepper
Sherry to taste

For the Julienne of Vegetables:
4 carrots
2 turnips
Salt to taste

To make the vegetable consommé:

Dice 3 lbs (1.5 kg) of the root vegetables.

Put in a saucepan with 4 pints (2.25 litres/ 8 cups) of water and the bouquet garni.

Bring to the boil, then simmer for 1 hour.

When the vegetables are completely cooked through strain off the liquid and leave to cool.

Take the remaining 1^1/$_2$ lbs (625 g) of root vegetables and mince finely together with the field mushrooms.

Mix together with the egg whites.

Add to the cold stock and mix vigorously until the egg whites and minced vegetables are well incorporated.

Put back on the heat and bring to the boil, stirring all the time.

Reduce to simmer and cook for about half an hour until the vegetable clarification is cooked out.

Pass through a fine sieve and muslin.

Add a little sherry and seasoning.

Serve with a Julienne of vegetables.

To make the Julienne of vegetables:

Peel the vegetables.

Cut them up into equal sized oblongs.

Slice very thinly.

Then slice in the opposite direction to make matchstick pieces.

Bring some salted water to the boil in a saucepan.

Add the sliced vegetables.

Simmer for about 10 minutes until tender.

Strain.

Add to the soup just before serving.

WATERCRESS SOUP

Dr Nicholas Culpepper recommended eating delicious watercress soup in his book The Compleat Herbal dated 1653. He writes: 'Watercress pottage is a good remedy to cleanse the blood in the spring, and help headaches, and consume the gross humours winter has left behind; those that would live in health may use it if they please; if they will not, I cannot help it. If any fancy not pottage, they may eat the herb as a sallad'.

8 oz (225 g) potatoes
2 onions
1$^1/_2$ pints (900 ml/ 3$^3/_4$ cups) chicken stock
Salt and pepper
2 bunches of watercress
$^1/_2$ pint (300 ml/ 1$^1/_4$ cups) milk
$^1/_2$ teaspoon nutmeg
4 tablespoons (2$^1/_2$ fl oz/ $^1/_3$ cup) single cream

Peel and slice the potatoes and onions.

Put into a saucepan with the chicken stock and season to taste.

Bring to the boil, and simmer until the vegetables are soft.

Wash the watercress; discard any thick stems or yellow leaves.

Reserve a few sprigs of watercress to garnish the soup.

Chop the remainder, and add to the saucepan.

Cook gently for a further 5 minutes.

Remove from the heat and allow to cool slightly.

Rub the soup through a sieve or liquidise in an electric blender.

Return to the saucepan.

Add the milk and nutmeg, and reheat.

Swirl in the cream before serving, either hot or cold; garnish with watercress.

ANGELS ON HORSEBACK

A savoury - excellent for today's buffet parties - which was very popular in Victorian times. Then it would be served, not as a beginning to a meal but to clear the palate before the pudding. During the Roman occupation, when Winchester was the fifth largest walled city in Britain and known as Belgarum, oysters found in Hampshire's river beds and around the coast were popular. During the Middle Ages monks were known to trade them for other goods.

24 rashers of streaky bacon
24 oysters, fresh or tinned
Anchovy essence
Lemon juice
Cayenne pepper

Remove the rinds from the bacon.

If fresh, take the oysters out of their shells.

Sprinkle each with a few drops of anchovy essence, lemon juice and cayenne pepper to taste.

Wrap a rasher of bacon round each oyster.

Place under a hot grill until the bacon is crisp.

Secure each one with a cocktail stick to a small piece of buttered toast or snippet of fried bread.

Serve very hot.

Mussels or scallops can be used in place of the oysters.

DEVILS ON HORSEBACK

Another popular Victorian savoury - which is rather less expensive to make today than Angels on Horseback. In Victorian times the oysters used in the Angels' recipe were cheap and plentiful, and the many oyster stalls and 'street criers' did a roaring trade. The term 'devil' refers to the hot taste of the mustard.

24 prunes
24 rashers of streaky bacon
Prepared English mustard
A little single cream

Soak the prunes and remove the stones.

Remove the rind from the bacon, and cut in half.

Wrap each prune in a piece of bacon.

Place under a hot grill until the bacon is crisp.

Secure each one with a cocktail stick to a small piece of buttered toast or a snippet of fried bread.

Serve very hot smeared with mustard and with a little cream poured over.

BAKED MACKEREL WITH GOOSEBERRY SAUCE

Serves 4

Mackerel with gooseberry sauce is traditional to the southern counties of England, particularly Cornwall. It is also a favourite in Hampshire. The delicious association of mackerel with gooseberries is said to date back to Norman times - ten centuries ago.

4 mackerel
Salt and pepper
2 oz (50 g) butter
The juice of half a lemon

Gut and clean the fish - when baking mackerel it is usual to leave the heads and fins on.

Score the fish with a knife on each side 3 or 4 times.

Lay the mackerel in an greased ovenproof dish.

Season with salt and pepper to taste.

Pour the lemon juice over the fish, and dot with butter.

Cover the dish with foil.

Cook in a moderate oven for about 25 minutes.

Baste the fish once or twice during cooking time.

Serve hot with gooseberry sauce.

Oven 350°F/180°C Gas Mark 4

FORDINGBRIDGE LAKE TROUT
WITH CUCUMBER GARNISH
AND FISH SAUCE
Serves 6

Trout in the lakes in Hampshire grow big, and the flesh is pink like salmon.

$2^1/_2$-3 lbs (1.25 kg-1.5 kg) lake trout
A little butter
Sea salt to taste
Black pepper
1 tablespoon chopped English fennel - or dill if no fennel is to hand
The zest and juice of half a lemon
Sprigs of fennel to decorate
Lemon to decorate

For the fish sauce:
1 wineglassful of dry white wine-use the same wine as is being served chilled with the fish
1 level dessertspoon of cornflour
A little cold milk

For the cucumber garnish:
1 cucumber
$^1/_2$ oz (15 g) butter

Gut the trout if necessary, leaving the head on.

Wash and dry the fish.

Cut off all the fins and vandyke the tail.

Cut a piece of aluminium foil big enough to wrap round the fish, and about 6 inches longer than the trout at each end.

Spread the foil liberally with butter where the fish will lie.

Put the fish on the foil and sprinkle with freshly ground sea salt, black pepper, the chopped fennel or dill, and the grated zest of the lemon.

Put the foil and fish on a large baking sheet.

Pour the juice of half the lemon and the dry white wine over the fish.

Fold up the foil to make a secure parcel, which will allow none of the cooking juices to escape.

Cook in the oven for 45 minutes or until the eyes of the fish go white.

Lift the trout carefully on to a warm serving dish, and keep hot.

Retain the cooking juices for the fish sauce.

Serve with cucumber garnish and decorated with slices of lemon and sprigs of fennel.

The fish sauce should be put in a separate sauceboat.

To make the fish sauce:

Strain the cooking juices left in the foil into a saucepan.

Put the cornflour into a small cup or basin, and mix to a smooth paste with a little cold milk.

Add to the fish liquor and bring to the boil, stirring.

Cook gently, still stirring, until the sauce thickens.

To make the cucumber garnish:

Peel the cucumber.

Cut into lengthwise quarters about 1 inch long.

Blanch the strips in boiling water for 1 minute.

Drain.

Melt the butter in a saucepan.

Add the cucumber strips and allow them to sweat, shaking and tossing them in the saucepan with the lid on gently for 2 minutes.

Oven: 350°F/180°C Gas Mark 4

DRESSED CRAB

1 medium sized boiled crab
2 oz (50 g) fresh white breadcrumbs
Salt and pepper
Lemon juice to taste
A little chopped parsley
Cayenne pepper

For the garnish:
1 hard-boiled egg
A little chopped parsley

Pull the shell and the body of the crab apart.

Remove the stomach bag from just below the head and discard.

Using a spoon, scrape all the brown meat from the shell and reserve in a basin.

Wash and dry the shell.

Remove and discard the legs and the greyish fronds known as 'dead man's fingers' from the body.

Remove the white flesh and reserve in a basin.

Crack the claws with a nutcracker and using a skewer take out all the white meat and retain with the other white flesh.

Reserve the small claws for decoration.

Mix the dark meat with the breadcrumbs, a little chopped parsley, lemon juice, and season to taste with the salt and pepper.

Pack the mixture back into the shell, leaving a space in the centre.

Flake the white meat and mix with the lemon juice, salt and cayenne pepper.

Pile the mixture in the space left in the middle of the shell.

To make the garnish:

Separate the yolk from the white of egg.

Sieve the yolk and finely chop the egg white. Mix together.

To garnish:

Use the egg mixture and the chopped parsley to decorate the crab.

Alternatively, dip the back of a knife into cayenne pepper, and use it to mark diagonal lines on the dark meat.

Serve the crab on a dish decorated with the small claws.

Dressed crab is traditionally eaten with a green salad and brown bread and butter.

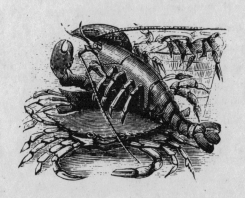

SALMON MOULD

8 oz (225 g) cooked salmon (fresh or tinned)
2 oz (50 g) butter or margarine
2 oz (50 g) flour
1 pint (600 ml/ 2¹/₂ cups) milk
Salt and pepper
A pinch of nutmeg
2 eggs

Rub the salmon through a wire sieve.

Melt the butter or margarine in a saucepan.

Stir in the flour to make a roux.

Cook for a few minutes, stirring.

Gradually add the milk, stirring.

Bring to the boil and cook for a few minutes, still stirring until the sauce thickens.

Remove from the heat.

Stir in the salmon and nutmeg.

Beat the eggs and add to the mixture.

Blend in a liquidiser, or beat thoroughly with a whisk until quite smooth.

Pour into a greased pudding basin.

Cover with a foil lid and tie down.

Stand in a sacuepan of boiling water.

Cover the saucepan and simmer for 30 minutes.

Allow to cool.

Turn out on to a serving dish.

Serve with shrimp sauce.

SALMON PUDDING

Serves 4

8 oz (225 g) breadcrumbs
4 oz (125 g) butter or margarine
2 tablespoons parsley, chopped
Salt and pepper
2 eggs
14 oz (400 g) cooked salmon (fresh or tinned)

Put the breadcrumbs into a basin.

Rub in butter or margarine.

Add the chopped parsley and seasoning.

Beat the eggs, and stir into the mixture thoroughly.

Use the breadcrumb mixture to line a greased pudding basin.

Break up the salmon with a fork into small pieces.

Put the flaked salmon in the centre of the pudding.

Cover with foil and tie down.

Put the basin in a saucepan of boiling water.

Cover the saucepan and simmer for 1 hour.

Remove the pudding from the heat.

Turn it out on to a serving dish.

Serve hot with a selection of vegetables or salad.

ROAST VENISON

Venison is the meat of the deer which have roamed for centuries in the New Forest. As venison is game, make sure it is well hung before cooking. Venison can be purchased, in season, from Hampshire butchers, particularly those in or around the New Forest. The haunch is best for roasting, but the loin, neck or fillet may also be cooked in this manner. It is advisable to cover the joint with a paste made from flour and water to prevent it drying out during cooking.

5 lb (2.25 kg) joint of venison with plenty of fat
Salt and pepper to taste
A little powdered ginger
8 oz (225 g) butter or more if required
Flour for dredging
15 fl oz (450 ml/ 2 cups) brown stock
1 oz (25 g) flour
A little lemon juice

For the paste:
3 lbs (1.5 kg) flour
Water to mix

To make the paste:

Mix the flour with sufficient cold water to give a stiff paste.

To prepare and cook the venison:

Dust the joint with salt, pepper and powdered ginger.

Roll out the paste on a floured board to about ³/₄ inch thick.

Melt the butter in a saucepan.

Brush the joint with some of the melted fat.

Cover the joint with greaseproof paper.

Cover the paper with the paste.

Place the joint in a roasting tin, and pour in the rest of the melted butter.

Roast in a hot oven for 10 minutes to harden the paste.

Reduce the heat to moderate and cook for a further 1 hour and 20 minutes.

Remove the joint from the oven, and take off the paper and paste.

Dredge the joint with flour.

Baste well with the melted butter, adding more if required. (Venison needs a lot of fat when cooking).

Return to the oven and cook for a further 20 minutes.

Baste frequently.

Remove from the oven and put the joint on to a warm serving dish and keep hot. Keep all the plates hot to prevent the venison fat from chilling and hardening, which it does very quickly.

Stir in 1 oz (25 g) of flour to the pan juices, and cook for a few minutes still stirring.

Gradually add the stock, stirring continuously.

Bring to the boil and simmer until the gravy thickens.

Season to taste with salt and lemon juice.

Strain.

Serve the gravy in a sauceboat, or pour round the joint.

Redcurrant or rowan jelly, or gooseberry sauce make an excellent accompaniment to roast venison.

Oven: 400°F/200°C Gas Mark 6 for 10 mins
Reduce to: 350°F/180°C Gas Mark 4 for 1 hr 40 mins

CASSEROLE OF VENISON IN BEER

Serves 6

3 lbs (1.5 kg) stewing venison
1 pint (600 ml/ 2½ cups) beer
3 oz (75 g) seasoned flour
8 oz (225 g) streaky bacon
A little fat for frying, if required
1 lb (450 g) onions
1 lb (450 g) carrots, thickly sliced
12 oz (350 g) mushrooms, thickly sliced
Salt and pepper
3 cloves of garlic (optional)
1½ oz (40 g) black treacle
1½ oz (40 g) dark brown sugar
½ pint (300 ml/ 1¼ cups) brown stock
1½ oz (40 g) redcurrant jelly

Trim and cut up the venison into pieces.

Marinate for at least 2 hours in ½ pint (300 ml/ 1¼ cups) of the beer, or sufficient to cover the meat.

Take the venison out and reserve the marinade.

Dry the meat and toss in seasoned flour.

Remove the rind and cut the bacon into pieces.

Fry the bacon in a frying pan.

Remove the bacon, and put it into an ovenproof casserole.

Fry the venison in the bacon fat to seal.

Peel and thinly slice the onions.

Fry the onions in the bacon fat, adding extra fat if required.

Remove the onions and add them to the casserole.

Add any remaining flour to the juices in the frying pan, and cook for a few minutes, stirring.

Gradually stir in the marinade, the rest of the beer, the stock, black treacle and brown sugar.

Bring gently to the boil still stirring.

Simmer for a few minutes.

Season with salt and pepper to taste.

Pour the stock over the venison in the casserole.

Add the sliced carrots, mushrooms and finely chopped garlic if liked.

Cover the casserole and cook in a moderate oven for at least 2 hours, or until the venison is tender.

Stir in the redcurrant jelly before serving.

Delicious with rowan jelly as an accompaniment.

Oven: 325°F/160°C Gas Mark 3

BROCKENHURST BAKED BREAST OF DUCK WITH APRICOTS
IN A PASTRY CASE   Serves 1 breast per person

8 oz (225 g) breast of duck
1 large onion
$^1/_2$ lb (225 g) fresh or tinned apricot halves
A little fat or oil for frying
8 oz (225 g) puff pastry
1 egg, beaten
$^1/_2$ pint (300 ml/ $1^1/_4$ cups) duck demi glaze sauce
Brandy to taste

For the demi glaze sauce - a classic rich
   brown sauce:
2 rashers streaky bacon
1 small onion
1 carrot
4 ozs (100 g) mushrooms
2 oz (50 g) butter or margarine
4 oz (100 g) flour
1 pint (600 ml/ $2^1/_2$ cups) meat stock
Bouquet garni
3 tablespoons tomato paste
Salt and pepper

Seal the duck breast in a frying pan and cook in a moderate oven for 2-5 minutes.

Remove from the oven and leave to cool.

Finely chop the onion and apricots and fry together for about 5 minutes, using the same pan as for the duck.

Leave to cool.

Roll out the puff pastry to approximately 12 inch square (30 cm) and as thin as possible.

Place a layer of onion and apricot mixture in the centre of the pastry, then the breast of duck, then another layer of onion and apricot mixture.

Fold the pastry case in an envelope fashion using the beaten egg to seal the edges.

Glaze the pastry case and sides with the rest of the beaten egg.

Bake in a hot oven for 8-10 minutes until the pastry is cooked to a crisp and golden finish.

Serve with the duck demi glaze sauce flavoured with brandy.

To make the demi glaze sauce:

Remove the rind and chop the bacon.

Peel and chop the onion, carrot and mushrooms.

Melt the fat in a frying pan, and fry the bacon for a few minutes.

Add the chopped vegetables and continue frying until lightly brown.

Stir in the flour and continue frying until the flour browns.

Remove the pan from the heat.

Gradually add the stock, stirring continuously.

Return the pan to the heat.

Bring to the boil stirring and cook until the sauce thickens.

Add the bouquet garni, tomato paste and salt and pepper to taste.

Simmer, stirring occasionally, for 1 hour.

Strain the sauce, return to heat and boil rapidly to reduce to about $1/2$ pint (300 ml/ $1 1/4$ cups).

Reduce the heat and add the brandy before serving in a sauce boat.

Oven: 400°F/200°C Gas Mark 6

TANDOORI CHICKEN FROM INDIA AND PAKISTAN

Serves 2

Tandoori cooking, which is becoming increasingly popular in the West, is a method of oven roasting or baking, which originated from the Punjab, in the north-west of the country, which was formerly India and now is Pakistan. Trade links with the east have existed for centuries, particularly through the international port of Southampton. Many visitors from abroad arrived at Southampton first. It is believed that Hampshire takes its name from Southampton, which was a town known as Hampton in the Middle Ages.

A tandoor is a clay oven, shaped like an Ali Baba jar, which is traditionally sunk into the ground. The food is cooked after being marinaded in spices on long vertical spits over a charcoal fire at the bottom of the tandoor. Tandoori style cooking can be improvised in western kitchens, and lends itself ideally to barbecuing over charcoal in the garden.

A 2 lb (900 g) very tender chicken
2 onions
1 inch piece of fresh root ginger
4 cloves of garlic, or to taste
1 green chilli pepper or $1/2$ teaspoon powdered
   chilli pepper
The juice of 1 lemon
$1/4$ teaspoon of salt
7 fl oz (200 ml/ $3/4$ cup) natural yogurt
1 teaspoon mixed spice
$1/4$ teaspoon ground cumin seed
A few drops of red and yellow food colouring
   (optional - a red colour is
   traditional to tandoori cooking)
Oil for basting if required or 2 oz (50 g) butter
A little fresh coriander or parsley

Skin the chicken.

Make several deep incisions in the flesh with a sharp knife.

Peel and chop the onions, ginger and garlic.

Chop the chilli pepper if used.

Pound the onion, ginger, garlic and chilli pepper to a paste in a mortar with a pestle or grind in an electric mixer.

Mix in the yogurt, spice, cumin and salt to make a smooth paste.

Add the food colour a drop at a time, and mix in well.

Rub the marinade into the chicken.

Leave for at least 2 hours at room temperature, or up to 10 hours covered in a refrigerator.

If a tandoor oven is not available, cook the chicken on a rotisserie at a high temperature, brushing with oil from time to time. Alternatively, roast in a hot oven for 30-40 minutes, dotting the chicken with small dabs of butter. Baste frequently during the cooking time, if the surface becomes dry.

Chop the fresh coriander or parsley and sprinkle on the chicken before serving.

Split the bird into two. Eat at once, while still very hot.

Traditionally tandoori chicken is served with a salad of thickly sliced onions, generously sprinkled with cayenne pepper.

Oven: 425°F/220°C Gas Mark 7

CHICKEN CURRY
FROM BOMBAY

Serves 4

The India Arms in Winchester dates from 1678. It is the only original coaching inn left in the City centre. The inn was the last stopping place for coaches carrying prisoners sentenced to deportation before they reached Southampton docks. Earl Mountbatten, the last Viceroy of India, gave permission for his coat of arms to be used in the inn sign, and a list of the Viceroys of India is proudly displayed in the pub, which of course, serves curry.

$1/4$ teaspoon ground ginger
$1/2$ teaspoon salt
$1/2$ teaspoon sugar
1 tablespoon coriander seed
$1/2$ teaspoon cumin seed
1 tablespoon poppy seed
$1/2$ teaspoon turmeric
A pinch of red chilli pepper
4 oz (100 g) butter or margarine
1 medium onion
1 shallot
1 lemon
4 chicken pieces
$1/2$ pint (300 ml/ $1^1/4$ cups) coconut milk
(This can be purchased from Asian food shops
or substitute $1/2$ pint (300 ml/ $1^1/4$ cups) cow's milk
with $1/4$ teaspoon coconut extract or essence)

Pound together the ginger, salt, sugar, coriander, cumin and poppy seed, turmeric and red chilli pepper in a mortar with a pestle or grind in an electric mixer, until they form a curry paste.

Peel and chop the onion and the shallot.

Melt 2 oz (50 g) of the butter or margarine in a saucepan and fry the onion and shallot with the curry paste, stirring continuously.

Skin and cut up the chicken into chunks.

Melt 2 oz (50 g) of the butter in a frying pan and fry the chicken until golden brown.

Add the chicken to the curry mixture.

Squeeze the lemon.

Gradually stir in the coconut milk and the lemon juice.

Bring gently to the boil, and simmer for 45 minutes.

Serve with patna rice and mango chutney.

RABBIT AND PORK HOTPOT

Serves 6-8

1 rabbit
1 lb (450 g) lean pork
2 oz (50 g) flour
Salt and pepper
1 lb (450 g) onions
1 head of celery
$^1/_2$ pint (300 ml/ $1^1/_4$ cups) milk
$^1/_2$ pint (300 ml/ $1^1/_4$ cups) meat stock

Cut the rabbit into neat joints.

Put into a bowl of boiling water to blanch for 3 minutes.

Cut the pork into neat pieces.

Season the flour with salt and pepper.

Dip the pieces of meat into the seasoned flour.

Peel and slice the onions finely.

Cut the prepared celery into small pieces.

Mix the onion and celery together, and put in a layer in the bottom of a casserole dish, reserving half.

Season to taste.

Cover with a layer of pork.

Arrange the rabbit joints on top of the pork.

Put the reserved pork in a layer on top of the rabbit.

Finish with a layer of onion and celery, seasoning to taste.

Mix the stock and the milk together and pour over the dish.

Cover the casserole with a lid.

Cook in the oven for about 2 hours.

Oven: 325°F/ 160°C Gas Mark 3

HAMPSHIRE ROLYPOLY OR BACON AND ONION ROLL

Serves 3

6 oz (175 g) plain flour
2 oz (50 g) lard
6 rashers of bacon
2 onions
Salt and pepper
Water to mix

Sieve the flour and salt together.

Rub in the lard until the mixture resembles fine breadcrumbs.

Mix in sufficient cold water to make a firm dough.

Roll out on a floured board to an oblong shape about $\frac{1}{4}$ inch thick.

Remove the rinds from the bacon.

Lay the rashers in rows across the pastry.

Peel the onion and slice thinly.

Cover the bacon with the onion.

Sprinkle with pepper to taste.

Roll up the pastry to form a roll.

Dampen the edges with water and press firmly together.

Put the roll into a well floured cloth and fasten securely.

Put the roll into a saucepan of boiling water.

Reduce to simmer, cover the pan and cook for $1\frac{1}{2}$ hours, taking care to top up the water if required.

This dish was traditionally served with mashed potatoes, mashed swedes and buttered greens.

BEEF, LAMB AND BACON CASSEROLE

Serves 5

This unusual mixture of beef, lamb and bacon in a casserole is traditional to Hampshire. In previous centuries farming for wool and meat was carried out more extensively in the county. At Weyhill, near Andover a famous sheep fair was held, which is thought to be the setting for Thomas Hardy's novel, *The Mayor of Casterbridge*, in which the drunken husband sold his wife and child to a sailor for five guineas.

12 oz (350 g) stewing steak
8 oz (225 g) stewing lamb
4 oz (100 g) back bacon rashers
2 onions
2 oz (50 g) flour
A little oil for frying
2 carrots
1 1/2 lbs (675 g) potatoes
Salt and pepper to taste
15 fl oz (450 ml/ 2 cups) brown stock

Cut up the beef and lamb into chunks.

Roll in the flour to coat.

Remove the rind from the bacon rashers

Cut the bacon into pieces.

Peel and slice the onions, carrots and potatoes.

Heat a little oil in a frying pan.

Fry the beef, lamb and bacon to seal.

Fry the onions until soft.

Put a layer of potatoes in the bottom of a casserole dish.

Continue with layers of stewing steak, lamb, bacon, carrots, and onions, seasoning each layer with salt and pepper, until the dish is full.

Fry any remaining flour in the frying pan juices.

Gradually add the stock, stirring continuously.

Bring to the boil and simmer gently for a few minutes.

Pour the stock over the casserole to just cover the meat and vegetables.

Finish with a layer of slightly overlapping potatoes.

Cover the dish with a lid.

Bake in a moderate oven for 2 hours.

To brown the potatoes on top, remove the lid for the last 30 minutes of the cooking time.

Oven: 350°F/180°C Gas Mark 4

HAMPSHIRE GAMMON
AND APRICOT PIE

Serves 4

A favourite very tasty regional dish that can be put in the oven, and forgotten about until it's time to eat.

8 oz (225 g) apricots
A 1 inch thick slice of gammon bacon, weighing at least
    1 lb (450 g)
1½ lbs (675 g) potatoes
Pepper
2 fl oz (3 tablespoons/ ¼ cup) water
1 oz (25 g) butter

If using dried apricots, soak them overnight.

If fresh apricots are used, stone and halve them.

Lay half the fruit in the bottom of a pie dish.

Remove the rind and any bones from the bacon.

Season with pepper.

Top with a layer of apricots, tucking the fruit down the sides and into any spaces.

Peel the potatoes and cut into ⅛ inch (3 mm) slices.

Put the potatoes in layers on top of the apricots.

Season the potatoes with pepper. Salt is generally not required as there is sufficient in the bacon.

Sprinkle the dish with the water.

Dot the top with butter.

Cover the dish loosely with foil.

Stand the dish in a large container to prevent the bottom burning during cooking.

Cook in a slow oven for 2 hours.

Remove the foil lid, and continue cooking for 20 minutes to brown the potatoes.

Serve with all the juices, either by itself, with vegetables or a green salad.

Oven: 300°F/150°C Gas Mark 2

ISLE OF WIGHT ROAST KIDNEYS IN ONIONS
Serves 4

4 large onions
4 lambs kidneys
A little kidney fat

Put the unpeeled onions in a saucepan of boiling water.

Simmer for 15 minutes.

Drain.

Cut a slice off the top of each onion.

Reserve to make a lid.

Scoop out the flesh from inside each onion.

Stuff the onions with the kidneys.

Put a little kidney fat on the top to baste the onions while cooking.

Replace the lids.

Wrap individually in foil.

Roast in the oven for 2 hours.

Oven: 350°F/180°C Gas Mark 4

HAMPSHIRE KIDNEYS
IN ONIONS

Serves 4

This dish is traditionally served in soup bowls. The kidney should be tender enough to eat with a spoon. In Southampton inns kidneys in onions were a popular supper dish for the many hungry sailors in the town. The rum was originally added by the men from their tot.

4 large onions
4 lambs kidneys
$^3/_4$ **pint (450 ml/ 2 cups) stock, approximately**
2 fl oz (3 tablespoons/ $^1/_4$ cup) rum or red wine

Peel the onions.

Cut a slice off the top of each.

Reserve to make a lid.

Scoop out the flesh from inside each onion, and reserve.

Stuff the onions with the kidneys.

Put the top back on each onion.

Stand in a casserole dish.

Pour on the stock until it comes half way up the onions.

Chop the reserved onion, and add to the casserole.

Cover the dish.

Cook in the oven for $1^1/_2$ hours.

Remove the casserole from the oven and add the rum or red wine.

Continue cooking for a further $^1/_2$ hour.

Oven: 325°F/160°C   Gas Mark 3

CARPET BAG STEAK
FROM AMERICA
Serves 4

Southampton is traditionally known as the Gateway to England. One of the largest ports in the country, it has always welcomed visitors from many lands. Links with America are very strong. It was from Southampton in 1620 that the Pilgrim Fathers set sail in two ships, the *Mayflower* and the *Speedwell,* to a new life across the Atlantic Ocean. The *Speedwell* had to put into Plymouth for repairs, and eventually the *Mayflower* set out on the brave adventure alone.

**2 lbs (900 g) rump steak about 1-1¹/₂ inches
  (2.5-3.5 cm) thick, cut into four portions
A small jar of oysters
Salt and pepper
Oil**

Using a sharp knife, cut a pocket in one side of each steak.

Drain the oysters.

Stuff each pocket with a quarter of the oysters.

Secure the pockets with small skewers.

Season the meat with salt and pepper.

Brush the steaks with oil.

Place in a pan, under a pre-heated hot grill.

Cook for about 5 minutes on each side.

This will result in medium steaks.

Allow less cooking time if a rare steak is preferred, longer if required well done.

Remove the skewers before serving with the cooking juices poured over the meat.

COUNTRY LEMON AND
STRAWBERRY CHEESECAKE

Cheesecakes have been popular for centuries in Hampshire.
Cheesecakes are traditionally baked in a pastry case. Strawberries
are probably at their best eaten on their own with just cream, but
they make a delicious topping for this cheesecake. William
Cobbett, author of the famous book *Rural Rides* farmed from 1804
to 1817 at Botley on the River Hamble. The rich soil of this area
makes it the centre of the famous strawberry growing region.

For the pastry base:
5 oz (150 g) plain flour
A pinch of salt
3 oz (75 g) margarine
1 egg
Cold water to mix

For the filling:
2 large eggs
1 lemon
8 oz (225 g) cream cheese
2 oz (50 g) caster sugar

For the strawberry topping:
8 oz (225 g) strawberries
2 teaspoons arrowroot
$^1/_4$ pint (150 ml/ $^2/_3$ cup) fruit juice or water
1 oz (25 g) caster sugar
2 teaspoons redcurrant jelly

To make the pastry base:

Sieve the flour and salt together.

Rub in the margarine until the mixture resembles fine
breadcrumbs.

Separate the egg, reserving the white. Beat the egg yolk.

Add the egg and enough cold water to mix to a stiff dough.

Roll out on a floured board.

Line a greased 8 inch (20 cm) sandwich or flan tin (a loose bottomed one is ideal) with the pastry.

To make the filling:

Finely grate the rind of the lemon and squeeze the juice.

Separate the eggs, and beat the egg yolks together with the cream cheese, caster sugar, lemon juice and rind, until smooth and well blended.

Whisk the egg whites, including the one reserved when making the pastry, until stiff and forming peaks.

Fold the egg whites into the cheese mixture.

Spread the mixture evenly on the pastry base.

Bake for 30 minutes until golden brown and set.

Allow the cheesecake to cool before turning it out of the tin.

To make strawberry topping:

Hull the strawberries and arrange them on top of the cheesecake.

Blend the arrowroot with a little of the fruit juice or water.

Put the rest of the liquid into a saucepan and heat gently.

Add the arrowroot.

Bring the mixture to the boil, then simmer until the syrup becomes quite clear and is of a thick coating consistency.

Stir in the redcurrant jelly.

Allow the glaze to cool slightly.

Spoon over the strawberries quickly, as it will set quickly.

Oven: 400°F/200°C Gas Mark 6

LITTLE CHEESE CUSTARDS

Serves 2

3 1/2 oz (90 g) cheese
1 egg
1/4 pint (150 ml/ 2/3 cup) milk

Grate the cheese finely.

Beat the egg and mix it with the cheese.

Bring the milk to the boil and stir into the mixture.

Pour into small fireproof dishes allowing 1 for each person.

Bake for 10-15 minutes.

Oven: 400°F/200°C Gas Mark 6

BRUSSELS SPROUTS
WITH CHEESE

Serves 3-4

A war time recipe used by Hampshire housewives.

1 lb (450 g) brussels sprouts
1 oz (25 g) margarine
1 oz (25 g) flour
1 pint (600 ml/ 2¹/₂ cups) milk
Salt and pepper
A pinch of nutmeg
2 teaspoons lemon juice
3 oz (75 g) cheese

Prepare and wash the sprouts.

Put in a saucepan with a little salted water.

Simmer gently.

Strain, and reserve the cooking liquid.

Grate the cheese.

Melt the margarine in a saucepan.

Stir in the flour to make a roux.

Cook for about 2 minutes, stirring.

Gradually add the reserved liquid and the milk, still stirring.

Bring to the boil and cook for a few minutes, still stirring until the sauce thickens.

Add the salt and pepper, nutmeg, lemon juice and grated cheese.

Stir to mix thoroughly.

Add the sprouts to the sauce, and heat through gently.

Serve hot.

CELERY IN CHEESE SAUCE

Serves 6

A large head of celery
$^3/_4$ pint (450 ml/ 2 cups) chicken stock
2 oz (50 g) butter or margarine
2 oz (50 g) flour
$^3/_4$ pint (450 ml/ 2 cups) milk
Salt and pepper, if required
4 oz (100 g) cheese, grated
2 oz (50 g) breadcrumbs

Discard the coarse outer celery stalks.

Wash, prepare and cut the celery into 1 inch (2.5 cm) pieces.

Bring the stock to the boil in a saucepan.

Add the celery and cover the saucepan and simmer for 15 minutes or until cooked.

Melt the butter in a saucepan. Stir in the flour to make a roux.

Cook gently, stirring for a few minutes.

Gradually add the milk, still stirring. Bring to the boil, and cook until the sauce thickens.

Strain the celery when cooked (reserving the stock) and put the celery into a fireproof serving dish.

Stir the stock into the sauce. Add the pepper to taste, and salt if required.

Stir 3 oz (75 g) of the grated cheese into the sauce.

Cook for a further few minutes, stirring.

Pour the sauce over the celery.

Mix the breadcrumbs with the remaining cheese.

Sprinkle the surface of the dish with the cheese and breadcrumb mixture.

Brown under the grill before serving.

BAKED TRUFFLES

Truffles are much prized as a delicacy. They are an edible fungus, which grows underground, often beneath oak trees. They have a strong smell, so both pigs, which are very partial to them, and dogs have traditionally been used to help locate them. They can be found in the New Forest.

Sliced truffles may be used to flavour gravies or sauces, in the same way as mushrooms. The truffle belongs to the mushroom family. Mrs. Beeton advises that truffles 'should always be eaten sparingly'.

8 truffles

Wash the truffles well.

Wrap each truffle in foil.

Bake in a hot oven for 1 hour.

Remove from the oven and take out of the foil.

Wipe each truffle on kitchen paper.

Serve hot as a vegetable in a napkin-lined basket or dish.

Oven: 400°F/200°C Gas Mark 6

HAMPSHIRE HERB PIE
WITH FRIED MARROW

Serves 6

Herb pies or puddings were traditionally an Easter dish, and included a variety of vegetables.

For the pie:
2 onions
3 cooking apples
1 lb (450 g) oatmeal
1 teaspoon honey
1 teaspoon chopped fresh mint (or to taste)
1 lettuce
1 leek
1 lb (450 g) spinach
4 oz (100 g) watercress
2 oz (50 g) parsley
$1/2$ teaspoon mixed herbs (or to taste)
4 oz (100 g) butter
1 pint (600 ml/ $2^1/_2$ cups) water
1 teaspoon salt
Oil for frying
1 lb (450 g) short crust pastry

For the fried marrow:
1 marrow
2 oz (50 g) butter

To make the herb pie:

Peel and chop the onions and apples.

Put in a saucepan with the honey and oatmeal and cook very gently stirring frequently, until the apples are soft.

Chop the mint, lettuce, leek, spinach, watercress and parsley.

Put the chopped green vegetables into a saucepan of boiling water - about 1 pint (600 ml/ $2^1/_2$ cups).

Simmer for a few minutes.

Drain and chop finely.

Mix with the oatmeal, apple, and onion mixture.

Stir in the herbs, butter and salt.

Fry in a little hot oil in a frying pan for a few minutes.

Roll out the pastry on a floured board.

Use to line a deep pie dish.

Fill the pastry case with the herb and oatmeal mixture.

Bake in a hot oven for 10 minutes then in a slow oven for 35-50 minutes.

To cook the fried marrow:

15 minutes before the pie is ready, slice the marrow into pieces about ½ inch (1 cm) thick.

Peel the rind from each piece, and cut out the seeds.

Melt the butter in a frying pan.

Fry the marrow until golden.

Oven: 400°F/200°C Gas Mark 6
Reduce to: 325°F/160°C Gas Mark 3

BROWN BREAD AND
HONEY ICE CREAM

This delicious ice cream used to be served in Winchester College tuck shop, and the recipe was a closely guarded secret. The famous public school was founded in 1382 by the Bishop of Winchester, William of Wykeham. It is one of the oldest in the country, and many of the original buildings remain today.

$^1/_2$ pint (300 ml/ 1$^1/_4$ cups) double cream
3 oz (75 g) wholemeal bread
1 oz (25 g) caster sugar
3 tablespoons ($^1/_4$ cup) thick honey
1 tablespoon orange or lemon juice

Take the crusts off the bread, and slice it.

Put the bread to dry in a slow oven for about 20 minutes.

Lightly whip the cream with the caster sugar.

Put the cream mixture into the freezing compartment of the refrigerator for 30 minutes.

Take the bread out of the oven when it is beginning to harden, but before it turns into rusks.

Crumble it on a grater or in an electric blender.

Melt the honey over a gentle heat.

Add the juice, and pour the honey mixture over the breadcrumbs.

Stir the sweetened crumbs into the semi-stiff cream, making sure that it is thoroughly and evenly mixed.

Freeze for a further 2 hours before serving.

(Note: There is no need to whip the ice cream during freezing, as it is low in water content. It is a requirement in many home made ice cream recipes to prevent crystals of ice forming).

STEWED PEARS IN RED WINE   Serves 8

Mrs. Beeton recommends leaving the stalks on the pears and using port wine.

2 lbs (900 g) pears
8 oz (225 g) sugar or to taste
$^1/_2$ pint (300 ml/ $1^1/_4$ cups) water or enough to just cover the
   pears together with the wine
$^1/_2$ pint (300 ml/ $1^1/_4$ cups) red wine
A few cloves
A little cochineal

Peel, core and halve the pears.

Put in a saucepan with the sugar, water, wine and cloves.

Simmer very gently until tender.

When the pears are cooked, remove gently so as to avoid breaking them and arrange on a serving dish.

Boil the syrup in the saucepan quickly for a few minutes until it reduces.

Allow the syrup to cool.

Add a few drops of cochineal to enhance the pretty pink colour of the dish.

Pour the syrup over the pears.

Allow to cool completely before serving with cream.

WINCHESTER PUDDING

A recipe from the *Harmsworth's Self Educator* dated 1906. In 1919 the poet John Keats wrote about Winchester: "It is the pleasantest town I was ever in".

In 1086 the Domesday Book was compiled at Winchester on William the Conqueror's orders. He wanted to raise taxes from his new kingdom and in order to do so needed to find out the local landowners' names, and how much each town, village and manor could contribute.

The Domesday Book stayed in Winchester for about 100 years and today gives valuable information about 11th century domestic life in England. Many villages named in the book can still be found in Hampshire.

3 oz (75 g) pudding rice (short grain)
1 pint (600 ml/ 2$^{1}/_{2}$ cups) milk
4 oz (100 g) raisins
3 oz (75 g) candied peel
2 eggs
2 oz (50 g) suet
2 oz (50 g) caster sugar
Grated lemon rind
$^{1}/_{2}$ teaspoon nutmeg

Wash the rice.

Put it into a saucepan with the milk.

Simmer very slowly (with the lid on the pan) until all the milk is absorbed.

Stone the raisins.

Chop the raisins, peel and suet.

Mix all the ingredients together.

Add the sugar, finely grated lemon rind and nutmeg.

Stir the mixture into the rice.

Have ready a buttered pudding basin.

Put in the mixture.

Cover the basin with greased paper and secure tightly.

Steam in a saucepan of gently boiling water for 2 hours.

Leave the lid on the saucepan, but take care that the pan does not boil dry.

Add extra water if required.

Turn the pudding on to a hot dish and serve it gently with any nice sweet sauce.

NELSON PUDDING
WITH APRICOT SAUCE

Serves 6-8

Bucklers Hard on the Beaulieu River was a centre of ship building 200 years ago. Many of the ships in Admiral Lord Nelson's fleet were built there. Today it is a centre for yachting and yacht building.

This recipe for Nelson Pudding is from a Brown and Polson Cornflour Recipe Book dated 1916, and priced one penny. The book states that the pudding costs 1s. 2d. to make! The company explain that Paisley flour is a type of baking powder so called because it was made at Paisley in Scotland. The name was changed to Raisley flour to avoid confusion with plain cornflour. Baking powder can be substituted, but a slightly smaller quantity should be used.

1 oz (25 g) Brown and Polson 'Patent' Cornflour
$^1/_2$ oz (15 g) Brown and Polson Paisley Flour (Substitute a
    scant $^1/_2$ oz (15 g) baking powder)
$^1/_2$ pint (300 ml/ $1^1/_4$ cups) milk
3 eggs, beaten
2 oz (50 g) Ratafia biscuit crumbs
2 oz (50 g) breadcrumbs or cake crumbs
1 oz (25 g) ground almonds
1 oz (25 g) chopped suet
$^1/_4$ oz (7 g) chopped lemon rind
2 oz (50 g) caster sugar
1 wineglassful sherry
1 few glace cherries
A strip of candied peel

For the Apricot Sauce:
2 tablespoons apricot jam
1 oz (25 g) caster sugar
4 tablespoons ($^1/_3$ cup) water
1 glass of sherry

Grease a plain mould with butter or margarine.

Put glacé cherries and candied peel in the bottom and up the sides to decorate when turned out.

Blend the cornflour with the milk.

Put in a saucepan, bring to the boil and cook for 1 minute, stirring.

Take off the fire, and let it cool for a few minutes.

Stir in the beaten eggs, the Ratafia and breadcrumbs (mixed well with the Paisley flour), the ground almonds, suet, lemon rind, caster sugar and sherry.

Place the mixture in the greased mould, and put in a cool place to set.

Turn out on to a serving plate.

Serve with apricot sauce.

To make the apricot sauce:

Dissolve the sugar in the water in a saucepan over a medium heat.

Stir in the apricot jam.

Add the glass of sherry, and stir again.

Allow to cool completely.

Serve the sauce round the pudding.

PUMPKIN PIE

Pumpkin pie is traditionally served on Thanksgiving Day in America. Recipes for pumpkin pie usually containing apple mixed with the pumpkin can be found in this country, dating back hundreds of years, so it is possible that the speciality first went over with the Founding Fathers. An annual Pumpkin Show is held at the 'Load of Hay' pub at Fordingbridge, on the edge of the New Forest.

1$^1/_2$ lbs (675 g) pumpkin
3 oz (75 g) brown sugar
1 oz (25 g) cornflour
1 lemon
A pinch of ground cinnamon
1 teaspoon ground ginger
1 teaspoon salt
2 eggs
$^1/_4$ pint (150 ml/ $^2/_3$ cup) milk
8 oz (225 g) shortcrust pastry

Cut the pumpkin into pieces, removing the seeds and outside skin.

Cook the pumpkin like a vegetable marrow. (Best put in a steamer over boiling water until very tender, approximately 15 minutes.)

Drain thoroughly, retaining a little of the liquid.

Mash well with a fork or blend in an electric blender.

Roll out the pastry on a floured board, and use to line an 8 inch (20 cm) flan ring.

Grate the lemon rind finely and squeeze the juice.

Beat the eggs together, and stir in the sugar, lemon rind and juice, cinnamon, ginger and salt.

Mix the cornflour to a thin cream with a little of the water the pumpkin was cooked in, and add to the egg mixture.

Mix with the mashed pumpkin, and blend well together.

Pour the mixture into the pastry case.

Bake in a hot oven for 15 minutes, then reduce the temperature and cook for a further 30 minutes or until the pastry is golden brown and the pumpkin filling set.

When cooked the pie may be sprinkled with cinnamon if liked.

If preferred, substitute ground nutmeg for the cinnamon, both in the pumpkin mixture and as a decoration.

Serve hot or cold with cream.

Oven: 400°F/200°C Gas Mark 6 for 15 minutes
Reduce to: 350°F/180°C Gas Mark 4 for further 30 minutes

LEMON FAIRY SHAPE

1¹/₂ oz (40 g) cornflour
1 lemon
1 egg
3 oz (75 g) sugar
³/₄ pint (450 ml/ 2 cups) water

Grate the lemon rind and squeeze the juice.

Put the rind and juice in a saucepan with the sugar and water.

Simmer for a few minutes.

Strain the liquid.

Mix the cornflour to a smooth paste with a little of the liquid.

Return the rest to the saucepan, and stir in the cornflour mixture.

Bring to the boil, stirring until it thickens.

Remove from the heat, and leave to cool a little.

Separate the egg.

Whisk the white until it forms peaks.

Stir it into the mixture.

Pour into a wetted mould.

Leave to set in a cool place.

Serve with a pint (600 ml/ 2¹/₂ cups) of thick milk custard round the fairy shape.

FRIAR'S OMELET

Serves 4

This is a delicious traditional Hampshire pudding made with apples, lemon and breadcrumbs. It is only people from outside the county who think it might be the other type of omelet made with beaten eggs.

1 lb (450 g) cooking apples
2 oz (50 g) caster sugar
1 lemon
2 eggs
4 oz (100 g) breadcrumbs
2 oz (50 g) butter or margarine
A pinch of cinnamon (if liked)
A little demerara sugar

Peel, core and slice the apples.

Grate the lemon rind finely and squeeze the juice.

Put the apples in a saucepan, with the sugar, 1 oz (25 g) of the butter, the rind and 1 tablespoon of the lemon juice.

Put the lid on the saucepan and cook very gently until the apples are soft. Remove from the heat.

Beat the eggs, and stir into the apple mixture.

Spread 2 oz (50 g) of the breadcrumbs to form a layer in the bottom of a greased ovenproof pie dish.

Cover with the apple mixture.

Melt the remaining 1 oz (25 g) of butter in a saucepan, and stir in the remaining 2 oz (50 g) of breadcrumbs and the pinch of cinnamon.

Spread the breadcrumb mixture over the apples.

Bake for approximately 25 minutes until firm.

Turn out and sprinkle with demerara sugar before serving with either cream or custard.

Oven: 350°F/180°C Gas Mark 4

BLACKBERRY AND APPLE PIE

Plate pies were traditionally glazed or iced.

8 oz (225 g) cooking apples
4 oz (100 g) blackberries
3 oz (75 g) caster sugar
12 oz (350 g) shortcrust pastry

For the sugar glaze:
Caster sugar to cover the top of the pie thickly
Cold water

For the icing:
4 oz (100 g) icing sugar
1 egg

Peel, core and slice the apples.

Roll out half the pastry on a floured board, and use to line a greased 8 inch (20 cm) pie plate.

Mix the apples with the prepared blackberries.

Pile the fruit evenly on the pastry.

Sprinkle with caster sugar.

Damp the edges of the pastry with water.

Roll out the remaining pastry and use it to cover the pie.

Trim the pastry, and press the edges together to seal.

Make a slit in the top of the pie for the steam to escape.

Bake for 45 minutes until golden brown.

To sugar glaze the pie:

Before cooking, brush the pastry top with water.

Sprinkle thickly with caster sugar.

To ice the pie:

Separate the egg.

Sift the icing sugar.

Beat the egg white and the icing sugar together until it is dry and forms peaks.

When the pie has been cooking for 35 minutes, remove it from the oven, and allow to cool slightly.

Spread the icing thickly on top of the pie.

Return to the oven, and cook for a further 10 minutes, or until the icing is golden brown.

Serve hot or cold with cream or custard.

| Oven: | 425°F/220°C Gas Mark 7 for 10 minutes |
| Reduce to: | 350°F/180°C Gas Mark 4 for 35 minutes |

HAMPSHIRE PUDDING PIE
OR GYPSY TART

Serves 6

Versions of custard tart are found in many counties, no doubt
inspired by the abundance of excellent eggs, milk, butter and cream
available. Some recipes include ground rice, ground almonds and
some add currants.

The Hampshire version is also known as Gypsy Tart. There were,
until quite recent times, a great many gypsies in the New Forest.
They were also known as Romanies or diddykies. They lived in
gaily painted caravans, and caught rabbits, squirrels and hedgehogs
for the stew pot. Many of the gypsies used to take timber from the
Forest to Portsmouth for use in shipbuilding.

8 oz (225 g) puff pastry
4 tablespoons strawberry jam
2 oz (50 g) butter or margarine
2 oz (50 g) flour
$^{1}/_{2}$ pint (300 ml/ $1^{1}/_{4}$ cups) milk
3 oz (75 g) caster sugar
Lemon

Roll out the pastry on a floured board.

Line a greased deep pie plate with the pastry, and spread it
with jam.

Melt the butter or margarine in a saucepan.

Stir in the flour, and cook for a minute, still stirring.

Remove the pan from the heat and gradually add the milk,
and the sugar.

Return to the heat and cook, whisking briskly, until the
mixture thickens.

Squeeze the juice from the lemon and grate the rind finely.

Add the rind and 1 tablespoon of the lemon juice to the
mixture.

Separate the eggs, and beat the yolks together.

Whisk the whites until stiff and forming peaks.

Stir the egg yolks into the mixture and cook for a minute.

Remove from the heat and fold in the egg whites.

Pour the mixture over the jam in the pastry case.

Bake in a moderately hot oven for 15 minutes or until golden brown.

Serve hot or cold.

Oven: 400°F/200°C Gas Mark 6
Reduce to: 325°F/160°C Gas Mark 3

ORANGE JELLY   Serves 4

This is a Victorian recipe. It has an interesting invitation at the end as well as a spelling mistake.

To make orange jelly take twelve China Oranges.

Squeeze the juice into a bason, grate the rind of one orange and one lemon.

Add two ounces of Isinglass to a pint of Water.

Boil it 'till it is quite dissolved then strain it into your juice.

Add to it half a pound of fine sugar (or to your taste).

Stir it often and when almost cold fill your moulds.

Mrs. and Miss Merry desire Compliments to Mrs. Russell and hope for the pleasure of her Company very soon to tea.

ORANGE CUSTARDS

Serves 4

From *The Experienced English Housekeeper For the Use and Eases of Ladies, Housekeepers and Cooks* by Elizabeth Raffald, 1769.

1 Seville Orange
1 spoonful of brandy
4 oz (100 g) caster sugar
1 pint single cream
4 eggs

Boil the rind of half a Seville orange very tender. Beat it in a marble mortar 'till it is very fine. Put to it one spoonful of the best brandy, the juice of a Seville orange, four ounces of loaf (or of caster) sugar, and the yolks of four eggs. Beat them all together for ten minutes, then pour in by degrees a pint of boiling cream. Keep beating them 'till they are cold, put them in custard cups and set them in an earthen dish of hot water. Let them stand 'till they are set. Then take them out and stick preserved orange on top and serve them up either hot or cold.

BOIL'D CUSTARD

Serves 4

The quantities and method are explained more fully above.

1 pint (600 ml/ 2¹/₂ cups) single cream
1 blade of mace
8 eggs
Orange flower water
Sugar to sweeten

A pint of cream: put it on a low fire with a blade of mace 'till it just boils, 8 eggs well beaten with a spoonful of Orange Flower Water. Sweeten it as you like. Mix it with the cream and stir it all of the while 'till it simmers, pour it into a basin.

OSBORNE PUDDING

The Isle of Wight has been popular as a holiday resort and has been offering good food to its many visitors since Queen Victoria made her seaside home at Osborne House in the 1860's.

2 slices of bread
1 tablespoon marmalade
$^1/_2$ pint (300 ml/ 1$^1/_4$ cups) milk
7$^1/_2$ oz (115 g) double cream
4 eggs
2 oz (50 g) caster sugar
1 dessertspoon of sherry

Cut the crusts off the bread.

Spread the slices with the marmalade and cut into small pieces.

Separate the eggs.

Put the yolks in a basin with the caster sugar, and beat well together.

Put the milk and 2$^1/_2$ oz (65 g) of the cream in a saucepan and heat gently.

Pour the milk and cream mixture over the beaten egg yolks and sugar.

Mix well together.

Cook the mixture in a double saucepan or in a basin standing in a saucepan of simmering water, until it becomes a thick custard.

Beat the remaining cream until thick.

Gently fold in the bread, sherry and the whipped cream.

Pile into a serving dish and serve chilled, decorated with either glacé cherries and angelica, crystallised fruit or toasted almonds.

HAMPSHIRE DROPS

Makes about 12

4 oz (100 g) plain flour
4 oz (100 g) cornflour
1 level teaspoon baking powder
4 oz (100 g) caster sugar
3^1/$_2$ oz (90 g) instant creaming margarine
1 egg
A little jam or butter icing

Sift the flour, cornflour and baking powder together.

In a separate bowl cream the fat and sugar.

Beat the egg and mix it into the creamed mixture.

Add the flour, and mix to a soft dough.

Turn the mixture on to a floured board.

Form into a long roll.

Slice the roll into ^{1}/$_4$ inch (5 mm) pieces.

Roll each piece into a ball, and place on a greased baking tray.

Allow room for the mixture to spread during cooking.

Bake in the oven for 10-15 minutes until lightly brown and firm.

Allow to cool on a rack.

Sandwich together in twos with jam or butter icing.

Oven: 375°F/190°C Gas Mark 5

MOTHERING SUNDAY WAFERS OR BRANDY SNAPS

Brandy Snaps, which are also known as Jumbles in some parts of the country, have a special name in Hampshire - Mothering Sunday Wafers. In Hampshire, the biscuits are traditionally made with orange flower water instead of brandy, and served with jelly. The tradition of wafers is strong in Hampshire. In Winchester Museum there are special wafer irons, which were used to make Chilbolton Mid-Lent Wafers.

3 oz (75 g) butter or margarine
3 oz (75 g) golden syrup
3 oz (75 g) caster sugar
3 oz (75 g) plain flour
$^{1}/_{2}$ teaspoon ground ginger
$1^{1}/_{2}$ teaspoons orange flower water or brandy (optional)
Half a lemon
Double cream to fill

Melt the butter, golden syrup and sugar in a saucepan stirring continuously. Allow to cool.

Stir in the flour and ginger and add the orange flower water or brandy.

Grate the rind of half a lemon very finely. Stir the rind into the mixture.

Put teaspoonfuls of the mixture on to a greased baking sheet allowing plenty of room for spreading during cooking.

Bake for 10 minutes or until golden brown.

Leave the wafers to cool for a moment, but while still hot and soft, roll round the handle of a greased wooden spoon.

Fill with whipped double cream before serving.

Unfilled brandy snaps can be stored in an airtight tin.

Oven: 350°F/180°C Gas Mark 4

ORIGINAL DOUGHNUTS FROM THE ISLE OF WIGHT

Makes about 24

2 oz (50 g) caster sugar
$^1/_2$ oz (15 g) yeast
$^1/_4$ pint (150 ml/ $^2/_3$ cup) milk
1 lb (450 g) plain flour
1 teaspoon salt
2 oz (50 g) butter
2 eggs beaten
24 teaspoons of thick raspberry jam

A little beaten egg to seal

Fat for frying

Caster sugar and ground cinnamon to dredge

Cream the yeast with the sugar.

Warm the milk until tepid, and add to the yeast mixture.

Leave on one side.

Sieve the flour and the salt together.

Rub in the butter until the mixture resembles fine breadcrumbs.

Mix the yeast and the flour mixtures together.

Add the eggs, and beat thoroughly to give a soft dropping consistency.

Knead the dough.

Cover the basin and leave the dough to rise in a warm place.

Knead again. Roll out on a floured board to about 2 inches (5 cm) thick.

Divide the dough into 24 pieces and shape each into a ball about 1$^1/_2$ inches (3.5 cm) in diameter.

Make a hole in each doughnut and insert a teaspoonful of jam in each, pressing the edges firmly together and sealing with a little beaten egg.

Deep fry the doughnuts for 5-10 minutes or until golden brown in very hot fat, putting 4 or 5 in a frying basket at the same time.

Turn once during the cooking time.

Drain well on kitchen paper.

Toss the doughnuts in caster sugar mixed with ground cinnamon.

The cinnamon can be omitted if preferred.

Best eaten the same day.

MRS FORSTER'S RECEIPT TO MAKE RICH SEED CAKE

From a 17th century *Book of Receipts*.

Take two pound of flower, two pound of butter, two pound of sugar, and a pound of Caraway seeds, mix together your flower, Seeds and Sugar and beat your butter up in a little rose water 'til it turns to cream again, then have ready very well beat twenty eggs, leave half the whites out, and stir your butter and eggs well together then put yr dry ingredients in a spoonfull at a time 'til all is well mixed, and keep it stirring 'til you put it into an Hoop. Set it immediately into a pretty hot oven if you put the rough sugar Caraways abate half a pund of sugar they do best. Add sweetmeats (Lemon, Orange and Citron) and ice if it pleases you.

LARDY CAKE

Different types of Lardy Cake are made throughout the country. Lardy Cake is still a popular tea time treat in Hampshire. The original Hampshire Lardy Cake was made without dried fruit and spice, so these ingredients may be omitted if preferred. However, when making Lardy Cakes pure lard must be used to give the traditional taste.

For the Lardy Cake:
$1/2$ oz (15 g) fresh yeast
2 teaspoons sugar
$1/2$ pint (300 ml/ $1^1/4$ cups) water
1 lb (450 g) plain flour
2 teaspoons salt
8 oz (225 g) lard
4 oz (100 g) caster sugar
1 teaspoon mixed spice
2 oz (50 g) currants
2 oz (50 g) sultanas

For the glaze:
1 tablespoon granulated sugar
1 tablespoon water

To make the Lardy Cake:

Cream the yeast and sugar with 2 tablespoons of the water warmed until tepid to make a paste.

Put in a warm place for approximately 15 minutes, until the mixture becomes frothy.

Sieve the flour and salt into a warmed bowl.

Warm the rest of the water.

Add the yeast mixture and the remainder of the water to the flour, and mix to a dough.

Turn out on to a floured board.

Knead until smooth.

Put into a warm place for approximately 1 hour or until doubled in size.

Roll the dough out on to a floured board to a rectangular shape.

Cut the lard up into small pats.

Mix sultanas and currants together.

Sprinkle one third of the lard, caster sugar, dried fruit and spice over the dough.

Fold the dough into three, sealing the edges with the rolling pin.

Knead until the ingredients are thoroughly blended.

Repeat this process twice more.

Roll the dough into an oval shape about 1 inch (2.5 cm) thick.

Put on a greased baking sheet and leave in a warm place for 30 minutes.

Bake in a hot oven for 25-30 minutes.

To make the glaze:

When the Lardy Cake is nearly cooked brush with the glaze made with one tablespoon sugar and one tablespoon hot water.

Stir the glaze over a gentle heat until the sugar dissolves and forms a syrup.

When removed from the oven, allow the Lardy Cake to cool upside down, so that the lard does not settle at the bottom, but is distributed equally throughout.

Oven: 425°F/220°C Gas Mark 7

CHOCOLATE SANDWICH CAKE

This type of cake (now known as a Victoria Sponge) was named after Queen Victoria, whose favourite holiday home was Osborne on the Isle of Wight.

3 oz (75 g) butter or margarine
5 oz (150 g) caster sugar
3 eggs
4 oz (100 g) self-raising flour
Salt
2 oz (50 g) drinking chocolate
1 tablespoon milk

For the chocolate butter icing:
3 oz (75 g) butter
6 oz (175 g) icing sugar
2 oz (50 g) chocolate
1 tablespoon water

For the chocolate glacé icing:
6 oz (175 g) icing sugar
2 tablespoons warm water
2 oz (50 g) chocolate

Cream the sugar and fat until light and fluffy.

Mix the drinking chocolate with the milk and add this to the cake mixture.

Gradually beat in the eggs.

Sieve the flour and salt together.

Gently fold in the flour.

Put the mixture into two 6 inch (15 cm) greased sandwich tins.

Bake for 25-30 minutes in a moderate oven.

Leave to cool in the tin before turning on to a wire tray.

Sandwich together with chocolate butter icing and coat with chocolate glacé icing.

To make the chocolate butter icing:

Beat the butter until light and creamy.

Gradually beat in the sieved icing sugar.

Melt the chocolate and add the water.

Mix thoroughly into the cream.

Use to sandwich the two cakes together.

To make the chocolate glacé icing:

Sift the icing sugar into a basin.

Melt the chocolate.

Gradually mix the water and the chocolate with the icing sugar to a smooth coating consistency.

Adjust by using more sifted icing sugar or water, if necessary.

Use to coat the top of the cake.

Decorate with chocolate strands before the icing sets.

Oven: 375°F/190°C Gas Mark 5

GINGERBREAD MEN OR HUSBANDS

In Hampshire Gingerbread men were traditionally called Gingerbread Husbands. These biscuits, still a great favourite with children, were sold at medieval fairs. They were originally made in wooden moulds. Today metal cutters are available. For special occasions gingerbread biscuits, especially those made in the shape of hearts as Valentines, were gilded. This is the origin of the saying 'taking the gilt off the gingerbread'.

8 oz (225 g) butter
1 lb (450 g) self-raising flour
8 oz (225 g) soft brown sugar
1 tablespoon ground ginger
2 teaspoons mixed spice
2 tablespoons black treacle
2 tablespoons golden syrup
2 teaspoons orange juice
A few currants or a little icing for decoration

Sieve the flour, ginger and mixed spice in a bowl.

Melt the butter, treacle and syrup in a saucepan, over a gentle heat.

Remove from the heat and add the orange juice. While still hot, stir into the flour, then allow to cool.

Turn mixture on to a floured board, and knead well.

Roll out, and make into gingermen shapes using a cutter or a cardboard shape.

Place on a greased baking tray, leaving a little room for spreading. Bake in the oven until firm.

Make the eyes, nose and mouth of each man with currants or alternatively with glacé icing.

(Note: Allow biscuits to cool for a few minutes before removing from the baking tray).

Oven: 350°F/180°C Gas Mark 4

ROSE HIP SYRUP

Hips are the berries of the wild or dog rose. They can be used to make a delicious syrup rich in Vitamin C. Two teaspoons daily would give an adequate adult requirement. Gather the rose hips when they are red and perfectly ripe.

2 lbs (900 g) rose hips
1 lb (450 g) sugar
4 pints (2.3 litres/ 10 cups) water

Coarsely mince the rose hips.

Bring 3 pints (1.7 litres/ $7^1/_2$ cups) of the water to the boil.

Put in the rose hips.

Simmer for about 5 minutes. Allow to stand for 10 minutes.

Strain through a jelly bag.

Bring the remaining 1 pint (600 ml/ $2^1/_2$ cups) of water to the boil.

Add the rose hip pulp and simmer for a further 5 minutes.

Allow to stand as before.

Strain through a jelly bag.

Mix the two amounts of juice together and put into a saucepan.

Bring to the boil, and continue boiling rapidly until the amount measures about $1^1/_2$ pints (900 ml/ $3^3/_4$ cups).

Add the sugar and stir until dissolved.

Boil for a further 5 minutes.

While still hot pour the syrup into clean hot bottles and seal.

Use small bottles, as the syrup only keeps for a week once opened.

GREEN TOMATO JAM

4 lbs (1.75 kg) green tomatoes
3 lbs (1.45 kg) preserving sugar
1 lemon

Plunge the tomatoes in boiling water for a moment, and then skin and cut into quarters.

Squeeze the lemon and grate the rind finely.

Put the tomatoes, sugar, lemon juice and rind in a preserving pan.

Bring to the boil, and continue to boil for about 1 hour, stirring frequently.

To test for setting point, spoon a little jam on to a cold saucer. Push the jam gently with the little finger, and if it wrinkles it is set.

When cooled, pour into hot sterilised jars and cover tightly with jam covers.

VEGETABLE MARROW
AND GINGER JAM   Makes about 5 lbs (2.25 kg)

4 lbs (1.75 kg) vegetable marrow - weighed after peeling
   and removing the seeds
1 oz (25 g) ground ginger, less if not too gingery a jam is
   preferred
3 lemons

Use only marrows that are ripe and yellow in colour,
otherwise the jam will not set or keep well.

Peel the marrow and remove the seeds.

Cut into small chunks.

Put into a bowl and leave for 12 hours or overnight.

Pour off any water that has collected.

Dry the marrow chunks on kitchen paper. Replace in the
bowl.

Pour the sugar over the marrow. Leave for a further 24
hours.

Grate the lemon rind finely and squeeze the juice from the 3
lemons.

Put into a preserving pan with the marrow and marrow
liquid.

Add the ground ginger and simmer for 30 minutes.

Bring to the boil, and continue to boil gently until the
marrow is transparent and setting point is reached. To test
for setting point, spoon a little jam on to a cold saucer.

Push the jam gently with the little finger, and if it wrinkles
it is set.

Allow to cool.

Pour into clean, dry 1 lb jam jars and cover tightly with jam
covers.

ROWAN JELLY

Excellent with venison.

6 lbs (2.75 kg) of rowan berries
3 pints (1.75 kg/ 6 cups) water
1 lemon
Preserving sugar-1^1/$_2$ lbs (675 g) to every pint
   of liquid obtained

Remove the stalks from the rowan berries and wash them.

Put the water and fruit in a preserving pan.

Bring to the boil.

Simmer gently until the berries are soft.

Allow to cool.

Put into a muslin bag, and let the liquid strain through into a basin.

To every pint of liquid obtained add 1^1/$_2$ lbs (675 g) of sugar.

Squeeze the lemon and add the juice to the liquid.

Return the mixture to the preserving pan.

Boil rapidly until setting point is reached - probably after about 30 minutes.

To test for setting drop a little jelly on to a cold plate, push with the little finger and if it wrinkles it is ready.

Allow to cool before pouring into clean dry jars.

Seal with jam covers.

RED TOMATO CHUTNEY

The tomato, regarded in the 16th century as an aphrodisiac in Italy and France, where the fruit was called ' pommes d'amour' or love apples, was neglected in the English kitchen until much later. The Elizabethans grew them only for decoration, but with the growth, towards the end of the 19th century, of greenhouses for cultivation in this country, tomatoes began to gain in popularity.

2 lbs (900 g) ripe tomatoes
2 large cooking apples
2 large onions
$^3/_4$ pint (450 ml/ 2 cups) cider vinegar
12 oz (350 g) demerara sugar
$^1/_2$ teaspoon cayenne pepper
$^1/_2$ teaspoon ground ginger
1 teaspoon ground cloves
2 red or green chillies
Salt

Blanch the tomatoes in boiling water for a moment. Skin them, and cut them into quarters.

Put in a bowl and sprinkle with salt. Leave for at least 12 hours, then drain. Put the tomatoes into a preserving pan (which has been rubbed with butter to prevent sticking).

Peel and slice the apples and onions.

Add the apples, onions, vinegar, sugar, cayenne pepper, spices and chillies to the mixture. Bring to the boil and simmer until the sugar is dissolved.

Cook, stirring occasionally, until the chutney becomes thick. Allow to cool.

Pour into warm, dry bottles and cover with jam covers, then with a round cloth brushed with melted candle grease, to make an airtight seal.

Store in a cool place away from the light.

LADY SEWELL'S YELLOW OR GREEN CABBAGE PICKLE

Found among remedies to drive away rats and mice, coughs and ague, and Cousin George's recipe to make black ink.

4 small winter cabbages
Salt
Garlick salt
$^1/_2$ oz (15 g) mustard seed
2 gallons (9 litres) vinegar
1 oz (25 g) termerick

Cut four small winter cabbages in thin slices, and then give them a boil in salt and water.

Spread them on sieves to dry.

Sprinkle a good deal of salt on them and set them in the sun.

Also peel a sufficient quantity of garlick salt and put it to dry for some time.

When both are perfectly dry have ready $^1/_2$ oz (15 g) of bruised mustard seed.

Then put a layer of cabbage into a jar and strew on some garlick and mustard seed, then another layer of cabbage and so on until it is all in.

Boil 2 gallons (9 litres) of vinegar with 1 oz (25 g) termerick and pour it on boiling hot.

WATERCRESS SPREAD

A savoury butter to use as a sandwich spread - excellent with ham, cucumber or cheese filling.

Hampshire is an important centre for the cultivation of watercress, particularly in the valley of the River Test. The watercress is grown alongside the river in stone beds, many of which have been used for generations. Ten miles of the old steam railway, the Mid Hants Railway known as the 'Watercress Line' has been preserved, and now takes visitors through the picturesque scenery from Alresford to Alton.

1 oz (25 g) butter
1 teaspoon watercress, chopped
Salt and pepper
Lemon juice

Wash the watercress well.

Remove any tough stalks and discoloured leaves.

Chop finely.

Cream the butter.

Add the chopped watercress.

Season with salt, pepper and lemon juice to taste.

APPLE BUTTER

This traditional country preserve was usually made when there was a glut of apples, as a large quantity of apples yields a comparatively small amount of preserve. It is an excellent way of using windfalls. Apple Butter was made in the famous novelist, Jane Austen's family. In a letter to her sister, Cassandra, dated 27th December, 1808, she remarks that their Apple Butter was not entirely solid, and was thought not to have been boiled long enough. Jane Austen lived in the tiny Hampshire village of Chawton from 1809 to 1817, where she wrote many of her famous novels, including *Emma, Mansfield Park* and *Persuasion*. It is believed that she modelled many of her characters on people she knew locally.

8 lbs (3.5 kg) apples (windfalls can be used)
1 pint (600 ml/ 2^1/$_2$ cups) water
4 lbs (1.75 kg) brown sugar
2 lemons
^{1}/$_4$ oz (7 g) ground cinnamon
^{1}/$_4$ oz (7 g) ground cloves

Peel, core and quarter the apples.

Grate the lemon rind and squeeze the juice from 2 lemons.

Bring the water to the boil in a large heavy bottomed saucepan (a preserving pan would be ideal).

Add the sugar and stir until dissolved.

Add the cut up apple, the ground cinnamon and ground cloves, the lemon rind and the juice.

Boil gently, stirring frequently to prevent sticking, until stiff and the consistency of thick cream. This will take from 3 to 4 hours.

Apple Butter can be potted into small jars. It improves with keeping for at least 1 year. Apple Butter is traditionally served at Christmas time, decorated with split almonds or hazelnuts and cream. If the Apple Butter is put into small basins or bowls to set, it can be turned out and eaten as individual puddings, decorated with nuts and cream.

BACON, CELERY AND APPLE STUFFING

2 oz (50 g) bacon
1½ oz (40 g) butter or margarine
2 oz (50 g) celery
2 cooking apples
4 oz (100 g) breadcrumbs (or 2 oz (50 g) breadcrumbs 2 oz
    (50 g) suet)
1 teaspoon chopped parsley
1 teaspoon dried mixed herbs
1 lemon
Salt and pepper
1 egg

Remove the rinds from the bacon and cut into small pieces.

Heat the fat in a frying pan.

Fry the bacon for a minute or two.

Remove the bacon.

Chop the celery.

Fry in the fat for 3 minutes.

Peel, core and cut the apples into small pieces.

Add the apple to the frying pan and fry for a further few minutes.

Mix the apples and celery with the bacon in a basin.

Stir in the breadcrumbs (or breadcrumbs and suet), chopped parsley and mixed herbs.

Season to taste.

Beat the egg.

Bind the ingredients together with the beaten egg.

Use to stuff pork, chicken or turkey.

GOOSEBERRY SAUCE

Serves 4

¾ lb (350 g) gooseberries
2 oz (50 g) sugar or to taste
A little water
2 teaspoons cornflour
2½ oz (4 tablespoons/ ⅓ cup) milk

Top, tail and wash the gooseberries.

Put the sugar with the water in a saucepan.

Stir over a gently heat until the sugar is dissolved.

Add the gooseberries and simmer gently until soft.

Rub through a sieve or liquidize in a blender.

Blend the cornflour with the milk, and add to the purée.

Return the sauce to the saucepan and cook gently, stirring until it thickens.

Serve with baked mackerel.

This sauce can also be used with lamb.

HOMEMADE TOMATO KETCHUP
OR CATSUP

1 oz (25 g) peppercorns
$^1/_4$ oz (7 g) cloves
$^1/_4$ oz (7 g) mace
1 oz (25 g) allspice
1 pint (600 ml/ 2$^1/_2$ cups) vinegar
7 lbs (3.25 kg) ripe tomatoes
2 Spanish onions
2 small onions
6 shallots
1 lb (450 g) demerara sugar
1$^1/_2$ oz (40 g) salt
$^1/_4$ teaspoonful of cayenne pepper

Tie the spices in a muslin bag and put it in a saucepan with the vinegar.

Bring to the boil. Remove from the heat, and leave covered to infuse for at least 1$^1/_2$ hours.

Slice the tomatoes.

Peel the onions and shallots and chop finely.

Remove the bag of spices from the saucepan.

Add the vegetables to the vinegar.

Bring to the boil and simmer gently until the tomatoes and onions are soft.

Rub through a hair sieve to remove the tomato skins and pips.

Return the tomato purée and vinegar to the saucepan.

Add the sugar and seasoning.

Bring to the boil, and simmer gently stirring frequently with a wooden spoon for 2 hours, or until sauce is very thick.

Allow to cool before bottling.

RED CURRANT AND RASPBERRY SAUCE

Makes about ³/₄ pint (450 ml/ 1³/₄ cups) Serves 3

A sweet fruit sauce to serve hot with Winchester or other plain puddings, or cold with ice cream.

¹/₂ **lb (225 g) redcurrants**
1 tablespoon water
2 oz (50 g) caster sugar
¹/₂ **lb (225 g) raspberries**

Put the prepared redcurrants in a saucepan with the sugar and water.

Heat very gently, stirring carefully occasionally, until the sugar dissolves.

Continue cooking slowly until the fruit is nearly soft.

Add the prepared raspberries, and cook slowly for a further two minutes.

Remove from the heat, and leave to cool.

Rub the fruit through a sieve, or blend in an electric mixer.

Strain before serving.

Heat gently if using to accompany hot puddings.

HOLLANDAISE SAUCE

Serves 4

This classic sauce of today, delicious served with asparagus and salmon, was known in the 17th century as 'butter sauce'. It is believed to have been a favourite of Queen Anne whose lead statue was given to the city of Winchester in 1713 to celebrate the signing of the Treaty of Utrecht, which ended the War of the Spanish Succession.

2 egg yolks
4 oz (100 g) butter
2 tablespoons (3 tablespoons) wine vinegar
2 tablespoons (3 tablespoons) water
Salt and pepper
2 drops of lemon juice

Boil the vinegar and water rapidly together until reduced to about one quarter of the amount.

Put the egg yolks into a basin, and stir in the cooled vinegar and water.

Cut up the butter into small pieces.

Add a piece to the egg mixture.

Place the basin in a saucepan of simmering water.

Whisk rapidly with a metal whisk.

As each piece of butter melts and is absorbed, add another until all is used, whisking continuously.

The sauce should be fairly thick in consistency.

Continue cooking until this is achieved, but do not allow the sauce to become too hot, or it may separate.

The sauce should be tangy and piquant, but if it tastes too sharp add more butter.

Add seasoning to taste, and stir in the lemon juice.

Do not heat again after the lemon juice is added.

WATERCRESS SAUCE   Makes about ¹/₂ pint

A delicious sauce with freshwater fish or grilled gammon.

¹/₂ pint (300m/ 1/¹/₄ cups) milk
1 small onion
4 oz (100 g) watercress
4 tablespoons (2¹/₂ fl oz/ ¹/₃ cup) stock or water
Salt and pepper
1 oz (25 g) butter or margarine
1 oz (25 g) flour
1 fl oz (1¹/₂ tablespoons/ 2 tablespoons) cream

Peel and slice the onion.

Put the milk in a bowl, and put the sliced onion in it for 30 minutes to flavour.

Discard any discoloured leaves and tough stalks from the washed watercress.

Put in a small saucepan with the stock.

Bring to the boil, reduce to a simmer, and cook for about 5 minutes until soft.

Strain and chop very finely.

Strain the milk.

Melt the butter in another saucepan.

Stir in the flour, and cook gently for 1 minute, still stirring.

Gradually stir in the strained milk.

Bring to the boil.

Reduce heat and continue cooking, still stirring until sauce thickens.

Stir in the watercress, the retained liquid and the cream.

Serve hot.

ELDERFLOWER CHAMPAGNE

Makes 1 gallon/ 4.5 litres

A traditional country recipe for a lovely summer drink.

1 lemon
3 fully blooming heads of elder flowers
1 gallon (4.5 litres) cold water
1½ lbs (675 g) sugar
2 tablespoons white wine vinegar

Squeeze the lemon.

Cut the rind into quarters.

Put the rind and juice of the lemon in a large container with the elder flowers, sugar and vinegar.

Add the cold water

Leave for 24 hours.

Strain the liquid, and bottle it in clean, screw-top bottles.

Keep for 14 days before drinking.

GRAPE WINE

1 quart (1.15 litres/ 4 cups) of bruised grapes
1 quart (1.15 litres/ 4 cups) of water
3 lbs (1.5 kg) sugar for 1 gallon (4.5 litres) liquor produced

Put the grapes in the water.

Allow to stand for five days, stirring twice a day.

Then strain it.

Put 3 lbs (1.5 kg) of sugar to 1 gallon of liquor.

It is to be strained for 2 or 3 days afterwards before it is put into a cask.

THE COUNTRY RECIPE SERIES

Available now @ £1.95 each

Cambridgeshire
Devon
Dorset
Hampshire
Kent
Somerset
Sussex
Yorkshire

Coming May 1988

Cornwall
Cumberland & Westmorland
Lancashire
Norfolk

All these books are available at your local bookshop or newsagent, or can be ordered direct from the publisher. Just tick the titles you require and fill in the form below. Prices and availability subject to change without notice.

Ravette Limited, 3 Glenside Estate, Star Road, Partridge Green, Horsham, West Sussex, RH13 8RA

Please send a cheque or postal order, and allow the following for postage and packing. UK 25p for one book and 10p for each additional book ordered.

Name..

Address...

....

....

Acknowledgements:

Grateful thanks are extended to the many people of Hampshire who have contributed towards this collection of recipes, including:

Pat Tattersall of Camberley, Surrey for Boil'd Custard and Orange Jelly.

Margaret Davis of Catisfield, Fareham for Hampshire Drops.

Barbara Newman for Gammon and Apricot Pie and local information.

Beatrice Osborn of Southsea for Hampshire Pie or Gypsy Tart.

Barbara Stickland of Winchester for Winchester Pudding.

Gillian Horn and Pauline Smith for help with research.

Helen Brown of Winchester for Brown Bread Honey Ice Cream from The Caterer at Winchester College and Apple Butter.

Grace Kingsnorth of Southampton from Hampshire Herb Pie.

Audrey Chalk of Alresford for Stilton and Celery Soup.

Valerie Atherton of Fordingbridge for Fordingbridge Lake Trout.

Audrey Martin of Lymington for Chocolate Sandwich Cake.

Hampshire Record Office for Grape Wine, Nelson Pudding with Apricot Sauce, Lady Sewell's Yellow and Green Cabbage Pickle and Rich Seed Cake.

Careys Manor Hotel, Brockenhurst for Vegetable Consommé and Brockenhurst Baked Breast of Duck.